T0297476

Cyclone Hart:
Wicked Left Hook

By Eugene "Cyclone" Hart

Book Designer: Angelica Cabias

To order additional copies of this book, contact:
Xlibris
844-714-8691
www.Xlibris.com
Orders@Xlibris.com

ISBN: Softcover 978-1-4257-5786-1

Print information available on the last page

Rev. date: 12/27/2021

The Eugene "Cyclone" Hart Story:

SESSION I: October 21, 2006

My name is Eugene Hart. I come up out of Philadelphia. I was born at Philadelphia General Hospital. I was born on June 16, 1951. My mothers name is Virginia Hart. When I was a young boy, my father wasn't there for me at that time. He had left town and went to New York and never came back. So it was just my mom and I together. Growing up without a Dad made my relationship with my Mom even better. We had a good relationship.

Spectrum Fights

When I came out of the hospital my mother and I moved into a house at 24th and Redman in 1951and we lived there until about 1965. We moved on from there and I went to middle school at 24th and Jefferson. I started middle school about 5 years old. I left middle school at 12 years old and I took my life a little further from there. I started boxing when I was 14 years old. I started boxing at the PAL (Police Athletic League) recreation center. It was called Columbia Avenue back then. It was Dukes PAL center located at 23rd and Columbia. When I started out in boxing I came up with a couple of friends of mine by the names of George and his brother who is another fighter named Bobby "Boogaloo" Watts. I went to the PAL center with George one day and I started my boxing career from there. We both started going to the gym together.

My mother met up with a man named Jessie Ryan when she was about 22 years old. I came up with a Stepfather. He did whatever he could do for my mother and me that made life a little easier. I accepted him into my life as my father. He has been a great support with my career. He's been a part of my career ever since I started and remained so until my career ended. He's really been a great father. He has remained a positive male role model throughout my life and today we continue to do things together. My Mom passed away in 2004. My father and I currently reside together in Philadelphia in which I try to be a great help to him since he has to receive dialysis treatments.

As a child we moved several times during my school days. I remember moving from 24th and Redman Street to 24th and Ingersoll Street and then from Ingersoll Street to 1833 No. Newkirk Street. I was there from about 17 years old until about the age of 32 years old, which was about the year of 1983. This was when I retired from boxing.

When I was coming up around the age of 11 years old we had a lot of problems in our neighborhood with guys that were fighting all the time. Fighting was the main way of surviving in our community. I wasn't the type of guy who wanted to be a fighter. I was more interested in trying to help the community and I would take up for guys whether they could fight or they couldn't fight if they needed help. It didn't matter. I just didn't like bullies; maybe that's why I became a professional fighter. I didn't really like the guys picking on the guys that couldn't or didn't know how to fight. Some guys were bullies and would take advantage of others that didn't know how to protect themselves. During that time they would try to force you in the gangs by beating you up before and after school.

EUGENE 'CYCLONE' HART
30-9-1 / 28 KO / 1 NC

YEAR	DATE	OPPONENT	RESULT	SITE	VENUE	RELIC
1969	Sep. 30	Shelton Moore	KO1	Philadelphia	Blue Horizon	POST
	Oct. 14	Sonny Gravely	KO1	Philadelphia	Blue Horizon	
	Nov. 11	Allen Thomas	KO2	Philadelphia	Blue Horizon	
	Dec. 9	Art Kettles	KO3	Philadelphia	Blue Horizon	
1970	Jan. 13	Sam Mosley	KO1	Philadelphia	Blue Horizon	POST
	Jan. 27	Joe Williams	KO1	Philadelphia	Blue Horizon	
	Feb. 25	Gene Masters	KO1	Philadelphia	Blue Horizon	
	Mar. 25	John Saunders	KO3	Philadelphia	Blue Horizon	
	Apr. 7	Vernon Mason	KO9	Philadelphia	Blue Horizon	
	May 18	Sonny Floyd	KO1	Philadelphia	Blue Horizon	
	May 26	John Saunders	KO4	Wilmington	Fournier Hall	
	Jun. 15	Humberto Trottman	KO5	Philadelphia	Arena	
	Sep. 16	Leroy Roberts	KO4	Philadelphia	Blue Horizon	
	Nov. 2	Humberto Trottman	KO2	Philadelphia	Arena	POST
	Nov. 17	Dave Dittmar	KO5	Philadelphia	Spectrum	
	Dec. 9	Jim Davis	KO4	Philadelphia	Blue Horizon	POST
1971	Jan. 26	Fred Martinovich	KO3	Philadelphia	Blue Horizon	
	Mar. 22	Jim Meilleur	KO4	Philadelphia	Arena	POST
	May 3	Kitten Hayward	TKO1	Philadelphia	Arena	POST TICK PROG
	Jun. 22	Don Fullmer	W10	Philadelphia	Spectrum	TICK
	Aug. 10	Fate Davis	KO5	Philadelphia	Spectrum	
	Sep. 21	Denny Moyer	NC6	Philadelphia	Spectrum	

List of Fights

I was never really like that at all and so I started boxing. I met a guy who became a friend of mine. His name is George Watts. We started going to the Duke center and this is where I started my career. It was a lot of neighborhood gangs at the time. Guys couldn't go from 24th and Redman to Demarco's at 23rd and Jefferson and all around there. There were other gang members over at Seybert Street. This is what was going on at that time when I was growing up in that neighborhood. So I chose another way to go because a lot of these young dudes were involved in gang wars and shooting guns and doing different things of that nature. I decided to go into the gym and do something better because I didn't like a lot of the guys that were doing the bullying and taking advantage of other young teens. Drugs weren't as involved at that time when I was coming up in the 1960's. At least they weren't as noticeable back then in the 60's as it is today. More things were hidden back then and we didn't know much about drugs. The activity wasn't as open as it is today. Now things that go on today are wide open and everybody knows about the drug activity. Nowadays, everybody knows what's going on, it's out there and a lot of people are involved. Back then it was hidden more instead of being out in the open and noticeable. I remember there were times when I used to see guys nodding and closing their eyes. I used to wonder why they were like that. I used to ask were they sleepy or was something going on. These were older guys that were nodding and I thought they were tired from working. Now today it's more open to the youth and a lot of the young kids today are more involved in it. So it makes me struggle harder with trying to change a lot of things that are going on in our community with drugs and the fact that now a lot of our youth are killing one another.

1972	Feb. 7	Matt Donovan	KO2	Philadelphia	Arena	
	Mar. 7	Nate Collins	KO'd 8	Philadelphia	Spectrum	
1973	Apr. 23	Jose Gonzalez	KO'd 9	Philadelphia	Arena	
	Aug. 6	Doc Holiday	KO2	Philadelphia	Spectrum	
	Nov. 12	Al Quinney	KO2	Philadelphia	Spectrum	
1974	Feb. 18	Willie Monroe	L10	Philadelphia	Spectrum	POST
	Jul. 15	Bobby Watts	KO'd 1	Philadelphia	Spectrum	POST
	Aug. 26	Eddie Gregory (Mustafa Muhammad)	KO'd 4	New York	Felt Forum	
1975	Jan. 31	Redames Cabrera	KO8	Philadelphia	Arena	
	Apr. 28	Mario Rosa	KO4	Philadelphia	Arena	
	Jun. 2	Jesse 'Chucho' Garcia	TKO6	Philadelphia	Arena	
	Aug. 15	Sugar Ray Seales	W10	Atlantic City	Convention Hall	
	Nov. 18	Bennie Briscoe	D10	Philadelphia	Spectrum	POST PROC
1976	Feb. 10	Melvin Dennis	KO3	Philadelphia	Spectrum	
	Apr. 6	Bennie Briscoe	KO'd 1	Philadelphia	Spectrum	POST
	Aug. 11		KO2	Philadelphia	Wagner Ballroom	
		Matt Donovan				
	Sep. 14	Marvin Hagler	TKO'd 9	Philadelphia	Spectrum	
1977	Mar. 11	Vito Antuofermo	KO'd 5	Philadelphia	Arena	PHO1
1982	Feb. 9	Tony Suero	KO'd 4	Atlantic City	Tropicana Hotel Casino	

List of Fights

When I was coming up as a kid I had polio. My legs weren't strong and they felt weak all the time. I wasn't able to run a lot so I started to do things that would build my body and my legs up so I could participate with the other youth in the neighborhood. I met a gentleman at the age of 14 years old. At this time I had started to walk a lot and build my lower body up. This is when I met Sam Solomon at the Champs gym at 24th and Ridge. He was the trainer of Ernie Terrell and Jessie Smith, two well-known fighters. Sam continued to show me ways to build up my legs. He used to put weights on my legs and this built me up to be successful as I am today in boxing. The main reason why I got into the gym was because of the fact that guys in the neighborhood would bully and try to take advantage of little guys and I wanted to be the type of guy to try to help those who needed help. My life has always been built around trying to help the other guys who were taken advantage of.

My career as an amateur was much better in terms of my legs. One day I met Georgie, Boogaloo's brother at 24th and Ingersoll. He said come on Hart; lets go to the gym for a workout. I took him up on that offer. In the gym I was able to build my legs by running and doing things like body-building. This really helped me perform a little better. So I stuck to the boxing and have been very successful since then. Sam Solomon was the guy who introduced me to doing things like working out and body-building.

During the time of my amateur fighting we would go out to different gyms and different areas to fight other guys. I remember going to Valley Forge with Boogaloo Watts, that's his name now, back then he was known as Bobby. We would get together and go to different gyms. Valley Forge was one of the main gyms that we would go to from the PAL center and fight. One of the main reasons we liked to go to Valley Forge to fight was because a lot of times when we went they had some good food there. We would go there and fight, but we had a chance to eat the good food they had. They would also give out rings and watches at that time. We would fight to get a ring or a watch or something and we were so proud of that. Earning something for our effort was what kept us going. Every center that we went to fight at was all PAL recreation centers. The centers were built for the young people in the neighborhood to be used for recreation to keep us occupied. Most of our fights back then were at PAL centers in different cities. We went to Wilmington, DE. and places like Vineland, NJ. We mainly fought at Valley Forge and Wilmington, Delaware. Bobby and George were good friends of mine at this time. George and I were closer in age so we hung together. They lived at the beginning of the block and I lived in the middle of the block. George and I would go to the Dukes PAL center at 23rd and Columbia together and when we arrived, Bobby "Boogaloo" was already in the gym. We were just following behind his footsteps and also trying to do something to help the youth in the community.

I turned Pro in 1969 at the age of 17. My first fight was at the Blue Horizon in Philadelphia. All my 19 fights thereafter, were at the Blue Horizon. When I started out, my manager was Sam Solomon. Then I went to New York and met a guy named Custamotto. I traveled with him for 3 years. He's the same trainer that had Mike Tyson. *END OF SESSION 1:*

Inquirer Photography by ROBERT M. TEEPLE

Hart VS Quinney

In 1965 I was preparing myself for the 1969 Olympics. I went to the finals and they cut me by disqualification because I didn't have enough points but because of my skill level I turned pro in 1969. This is where my career took off. Sugar Ray Seales was fighting in the Olympics as I was preparing for the Olympics. Somewhere down the line in 1975, I actually fought against Seales and won.

The fight with Freddie Martinovich on Dec 9th, 1970 was really nothing to talk about. I knocked him out in the 2nd round. He was in the way of me winning the championship title. I had to move him out of the way. He was more like a stepping-stone to get to the championship. I looked at it like I looked at all of my other opponents. I was looking at it in terms of going to the next level. I had to step up my game if I was going to be the champion of the world. The guys weren't lasting for more than 2-3 rounds as in my other 19 fights. I was doing 4 rounds at the time. Then around my eighth fight, I went from six 4 rounders to 8 rounds. After 2 eight round fights I started doing 10 round fights. I was fighting guys that would eventually build me up to go against better fighters.

It was November 2, 1970 I remember when I went against Humberto Trotman. I heard a lot of talk about how great a puncher he was. How tough he was. It was a good fight. I stopped him in the first round with a TKO with a body shot. I was knocking them out in the first 2 to 3 rounds. I was taking them out right away. These fights were like steppingstones and these fighters were more so in the way. Guys that wanted to be Champion of the World had to remove those guys who were in their way. Most of the guys that I boxed with, I looked at them as being in my way. When I boxed the guys in the gym by sparring, they were more treacherous then they guys I was fighting in the ring. Most of the fights that I had in the gyms were wars. We had top-notch fighters that we sparred with. That means you rather fight him than to spar with him because you want to get money with him. You knew this would be a great fight. So these fighters from the gym is what helped condition me for my fights so I knew how to get them out of the ring quickly. My gift was the wicked left hook to the body.

For a time I was fighting every two weeks. I would fight in Philadelphia and train in New York. When I fell out of the ring that was during the fight of Denny Moyer in 1971. From 1969 to 1971 was the highlight of my fighting career. March 22, 1971 I fought Jimmy Meilleur. My fight with Stan Kitten Hayward was on May 3, 1971 and in September of 1971 I fought Denny Moyer. After I fell out of the ring with Denny Moyer I took on another trainer and moved to New York to see what else I could learn to help prepare me for the latter part of my career. I took a break until 1973. I got caught up into some things in N.Y. and I came back to Philly and reunited with my first manager Sam Solomon. Sam Solomon was a great and knowledgeable trainer who helped me to become a good puncher and taught me how to become a great knock out artist. When I fought Willie the Worm I was with Custamotto in upstate New York. In 1971 after I fell out of the ring with Denny Moyer, I trained in the boxing camp with Custamotto from the end of 1971 to 1974-75 in the Catskill Mountains. Bill Clayton was my assistant manager, Jim Jacobs was my manager and Custamotto was my trainer. At the time Custamotto was training Ford Patterson. He also trained Mike Tyson down the line some years after my career was over. I've only known two professional boxers that gained the title belt and continued to win 19 straight knock out fights with no losses. They are Mike Tyson and myself.

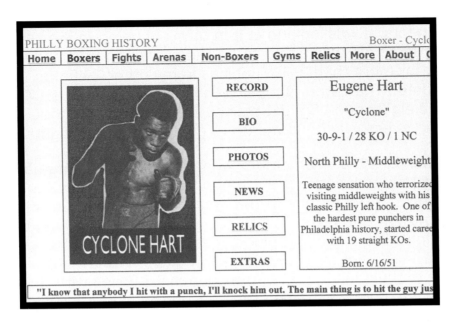

RECORD

BIO

PHOTOS

NEWS

RELICS

EXTRAS

CYCLONE HART

Eugene Hart

"Cyclone"

30-9-1 / 28 KO / 1 NC

North Philly - Middleweight

Teenage sensation who terrorized visiting middleweights with his classic Philly left hook. One of the hardest pure punchers in Philadelphia history, started career with 19 straight KOs.

Born: 6/16/51

"I know that anybody I hit with a punch, I'll knock him out. The main thing is to hit the guy jus

As a kid I had polio

Good Ole Joe:

I liked Joe Frazier because I was always amazed at how he would go in the ring and get off and not wait for the guy to punch him. He would punch the guy first. He was always putting the pressure on them. I was like Joe, I always liked to put pressure on the other guy and take them out. I would come out of the gym from training and my goal would be to get rid of my opponents right away. I always wanted to hit the other guy before he could hit me. I had learned from coming up in my amateur days some guys would get hit a lot and after the years they experienced a lot of broken ears, noses and hands and I didn't want to come up like that. I wanted to be able to hit the opponent more than he hit me so that I would be around for a long time. So my theory was to get off first.

I had to do my thing first and then worry about what ever happens later on. I wasn't worried about what was going on while I fighting because I wanted to get it over right away. I always took an aggressive stance to go out there and get off first by knocking my opponent out. I was a great puncher and an outstanding left hooker. So Joe Frazier in my book is the Worlds Heavyweight Champion of all times. He may not be to everybody else but he is to me. I admired him so much when I was coming up. He has a gym right there on Broad and Glenwood in Philadelphia. I studied his style and technique and used a combination of my and his skills. I used his aggressiveness and I used my own power and the gift of the left hook and this is when all the knockouts started. I also admire Cassius Clay now known as Muhammad Ali. Ali and Frazier had two different boxing styles. I like both of their styles. Muhammad Ali was a boxer and Joe Frazier was a fighter. They both encouraged me in my earlier days of when I first started out in the gym.

He's the only one that I actually studied but really my style developed from when I was a child with polio. I trained and punched on the heavy bag, I learned to develop a left hook on the heavy bag like Joe Frazier. He had a good left hook and a good right hand. He was always an aggressive fighter. So I was an aggressive fighter and learned this from when I was an amateur. I remember during the times that I would fight the crowd would roar every time I threw one out. It was like they would wait for that exciting left hook. It was like a tornado coming through. It was outstanding. A lot of times back then, I was a great drawing card. So the crowd would come see the great left hook. That's what I was known as, the best left hook. They knew that they would be coming to see a good fight. My opponent might not be around long but it was a good fight. People would say, don't go get a hotdog. If you come back the fight might be over if he throws that left hook. You don't want to miss it.

I didn't start fighting ten rounds until I went up against guys like Willie the Worm and Bennie Briscoe. I fought 10 round decision fights to get more money and increase my ratings in my career. It was guys that were up in the ratings when I started doing 10 rounds. The young guys that I started out with I took them all out in the first 1 or 2 rounds. On December 9, 1970 I fought Freddie Martinovich. I took on Stan Kitten Haywood. He was the first stepping stone in my career. He was an upgraded opponent that would allow me to make more money in boxing. I would make more money fighting him, than I would if I fought guys that weren't in the ratings.

At that time I was paid $50.00 for 4 rounds of boxing. I fought about 6 or 7 four round fights at $50.00 per fight. I had one six round fight at $175.00 and a couple of 8 rounders at $450.00 each and then I moved up to 10 rounds which paid me about $1,600 - $2,000 per fight. I only earned a few more dollars as each of the rounds increased. This was not a lot of money. For today's fighters the pay is outstanding compared to what we made back then. If you fought guys like Willie the Worm Monroe and other good rated fighters like Kitten Hayward that's when more money came into play because of the opponent that you fought would bring you a bigger purse. They were mainly those that had good names and had good boxing records.

Valley Forge and Delaware were the main two places that we dealt with at this time. We also went to Vineland, NJ. It was in Wilmington, Delaware that I got my name. As I stepped out into the center of the ring with the other fighter, I was given the name of Eugene "Cyclone" Hart by a referee and ever since then the name stuck with me. I carried the name from Wilmington, Delaware and it will stick with me for the rest of my life.

I had a lot of people that recognized my name. My trainer had a lot of friends who were politicians. When I started out with Sam Solomon he introduced me to a guy named Lucien Blackwell. He was over at 40th and Walnut at the time. My trainer would take me over to his house and we used to sit and talk about certain things pertaining to life and boxing being that he was once a boxer himself.

He was always a part of my life and career as I was growing up and I have always carried Lucien in my heart. When I met him I was about 14 years old. Lucien started coming to my fights and was an active participant in my life at this time and continued to do so. When I would fight, Lucien would say, "Hey Champ, you're going to be alright, just continue to stay in shape."

Hart VS Martinovich

At that time I believe Lucien was the President of the Waterfront. Then he started talking of becoming Councilman. He later accomplished this goal during the time of my career. I believe that Lucien and Sam Solomon were working with Ernie Terrell at the time. Ernie Terrell was a great heavyweight fighter. He fought Muhammad Ali, known as Cassius Clay then before his name became Muhammad Ali. The majority of things I learned about giving respect in my younger days were from Lucien Blackwell and also from Sam Solomon.

Jannie Blackwell is the late Lucien Blackwell's wife. Today she holds the position as City Councilwoman. I remember meeting Jannie at City Hall. Lucien was Councilman of West Philadelphia at this time. His office was located at 15th and Walnut. Occasionally, we would meet at his office and he would call Jannie at City Hall and say, "Hey Jane, Do you know that I have Cyclone Hart in my office?" Those were the good ole'days. In addition to Lucien and Jannie Blackwell, other influential friends who happen to be politicians like the Philadelphia Mayor, Mr.

John Street, and Darryl Clark, North Philadelphia's City Councilman, whom I had the pleasure of meeting during the Mayors first 4 years in office, Tommy Blackwell, Lucien's' son who is now North and West Philadelphia's State Representative has been a great influence in my career as a boxing trainer, advocate and educator. Lucien was the catalyst that started my wheels in gear about the program idea of wanting to keep the legacy of the boxing sport prevalent in today's youth. This is how I got involved in boxing at the Martin Luther King center because I had the help of Lucien and the local politicians.

At the MLK center, I work with youth and take them off the street and give them a couple of hours to free themselves of what's going on in the world today. There are a lot of things out there in the world more so now that can harm them, so I try to bring them in from the streets and give them something to look forward to in the near future and help them make a success of their lives. The boxing program is only one type of support, the other type of support is to help them change their minds about being caught up in the streets with war and guns by offering them life enhancing skills and an outlet to express what they feel. The boxing program runs from Monday thru Saturday, 5-9 pm. These hours are the timeframes that we keep the youth off the street. The War on Guns, Stop the Violence gives incentives for our youth who participate. At the age of 14 years old some of the children are eligible for jobs. We hire them in the summer. Making money is always a motivating factor and keeps them occupied while they learn life skills. *END OF SECOND SESSION:*

SESSION THREE: November 4, 2006

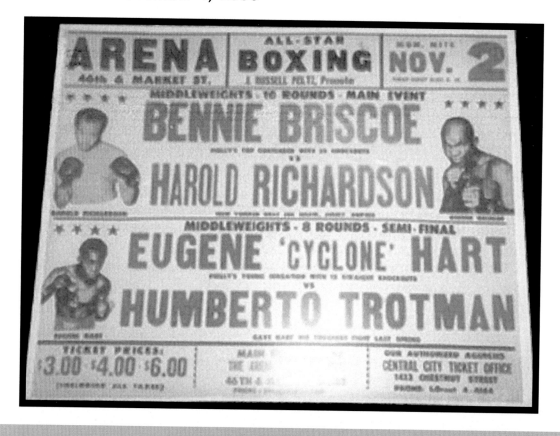

When I started the Lucien Blackwell boxing program I thought about how kids could wind up being champions of our city and that they would wear the Lucien Blackwell belts. I put that together to see if we could develop these kids into champions in the remembrance of Lucien. I am going behind a great legacy of a champion in my life, Lucien Blackwell. Lucien was my mentor, an amateur golden glove boxer, and his boxing career is what inspired me to want to bring the youth together to make them champions and to give them a Lucien Blackwell Championship belt to wear in honor of Lucien's memory and to keep his legacy of setting goals and accomplishing these goals. The fighters would be proud to wear the Lucien Blackwell belt. Lucien would tell me about a lot of things that he learned and experienced when he was boxing and he passed it on to me and I in turn pass it on to the youth that I mentor today. So now that a great guy such as Lucien instilled this information I have been given something to work with. Some of the youth in the program today are far removed from Lucien because they have never heard of him as a boxer and know nothing about his career and accomplishments, so I tell them about Lucien and about his drive and motivation to become president of the Waterfront and then later become a city politician, so he was a champion in many different aspects because he wore a lot of hats. When I speak to the youth about Lucien I express to them that I want them to become the same type of role model for other youth behind them as Lucien was for me.

When you look at the way the kids are coming up today you realize they are coming up without a mother, father or sometimes without both present. I truly think that I should be a part of straightening out what they are into today. I need to be a part of keeping the guns off the street and giving them a better of life. I want to show them that there is a difference in life when you choose to get involved with things that are more important than standing on the corner, shooting and killing one another. I wanted to be a part of that so I took off my boxing shoes at the time I retired in 1983 and I am back to help the youth to fight and stop the war on guns and stop the violence. I want to put my boxing skills out there and impart it to them to help take off the frustration of every day living and stresses they face today. This is what they need. A lot of times kids are looking for love in all the wrong places. Sometimes we down rate our kids and tell them that they aren't this or that. But if we put some time into our kids and grab a hold of our kids and let them know that we love them and that we want to do something to help, it might change the mindset of the kids that want to go out and shoot guns. So I have to be involved to help change their way of thinking. For the kids in the program, I take the time to train them. Most kids like my concept of training and how I deal with them. I would like to think of myself as a good role model for young boys and girls. I had two young ladies that I trained. One young lady named Dedrah came to the gym to train and she never missed a day in 8 months straight. She was really into what she was doing. She was focused.

Hart VS Moyer

When I started the Lucien Blackwell program at Martin Luther King Recreation Center   it was because Lucien inspired me during my boxing career.   Now I want to pass on his legacy to the youth so they can feel proud and comfortable regarding the sport of boxing. I want to give them the chance to proudly wear a Lucien Blackwell belt. This is definitely something to be proud of.   Lucien was a very important and well respected man who was a part of this great city and I am proud of him.   That's why it is important for the kids to understand his contribution to the city and all that he has done and accomplished. They will be honored to wear his belt.   I want to thank Jannie Blackwell, his wife and Tommy Blackwell, his son for being a great help to our youth. They are doing a great job with me with this program. I want to also thank the Mayor, John Street who is doing a great job in our city. I also want to thank Connie Little, Mayor John Street's secretary. This help inspires me to continue to move forward with the boxing program because we are getting a lot of help from the politicians in the city. Things go on in this city that are dangerous for our children and they help make it possible for me to get them off the streets. I only wish for Peace, Love and Happiness for our people everywhere. *END OF THIRD SESSION:*

FOURTH SESSION: November 18, 2006

I must say that from 1964 on to this day, my career has been great. I've been in the boxing game from age 14 and retired at age 32 in1983. Today I use what was put in me through boxing and I give this back to the children today. My goal is to take the children off the street and give them a better life as they come up in the world from the streets. A lot of times the kids that come up in the world they don't get a chance to travel and see other parts of the world. When I was younger, I wanted to find out how I could travel the world. I went to different gyms and it helped me to gain status around the world. I had a chance to travel on airplanes and to get around to other countries and places. Boxing did this for me. I also wanted to travel and I couldn't afford to travel like I wanted to but boxing allowed me this luxury.

I'm dealing with my son and participating in his boxing career. I am watching him grow in the sport. It is not just about him. It goes deeper and beyond him. It's about all of the youth today. There is so much violence going on today in our city I am trying to do everything I can to bring the youth up in the proper perspective and give them a chance to experience what I did. I want to give them the opportunity to travel and see other parts of the world. I want them to have more opportunity because opportunity is out there if you are willing to grab for it. I'm trying to get them involved in boxing so they can get away from the guns and stop the violence so they can better their lives.

Hart VS Meilleur

In 1983 upon my retirement I thought that I was done. However, no sooner than I took off my gloves and shoes I had to put them back on. The things going on today has brought me out of retirement. I thought I would be done with work but as long as there is a war on guns, I am not coming out of retirement. I did this so I can help bring back our youth and contribute to their upbringing. It's not like it was when I was coming up. In my early days if you did something wrong, the other neighbors and parents in the community used to beat us even before we made it home to our mothers. They were more secure with the family background and the neighborhood. Then when we got home, well you know how the rest went. We don't have that anymore today. This is part of what is wrong with our communities and children. Children need to know that there is someone watching and that they have to be accountable for their actions and behavior. As parents, we must help change the conditions of our youth.

When we look at the current issues in our communities today, what gets us into trouble is money and what can get us out of it is money. What we need today is to put programs in place to help better our youth and give them a better way of looking at life. I say this because what we need for our youth are programs.

We need programs in this city to help change the mindsets of these children. We need to bring back the brotherly love to our city by people who will reach out and help support our youth. There has been recent talk and developments regarding the casinos. The casinos will provide job opportunities for some of the youth and their families. Hopefully, this will help some families survive. To live in this city you need a job. We can't go on living in this city with nothing to go on. We have to have hope somewhere. The only way we can make things better is for us to get together and have an action plan. Everyone needs to be a part of this if we are going to fix this mess we are in. A lot of the problems going on in our city, we have created a lot of these things on our own. Our children are on Ritalin, on SSI, children are being raised up in homes in which their parents or guardians are involved with drugs and they have seen this for most of their lives. The older people need to sit down and talk about how we are going to clean up this mess. The only way we can handle this situation and clean it up is money. The things that have gotten us into trouble is about money and we need money to clean it up.

We need to look at the issue of nutrition. Children can't learn without food in their bodies. Some have no food in their homes and there is no father around to say anything to them or a mother to help them. We have to go back to the basics. Today we don't have children being raised by two parents. They are practically raising themselves, coming up on their own. They don't have the guidance that we had. We had people to guide us through our lives to make us who we are today. Today we have children whose mother may be on welfare. They get a welfare check and the children eat noodles everyday. SSI has our children on psyche or behavioral medications and they go to school high all the time. The things that we create around our children we have to accept responsibility and take it away from them in order to give them a better life. We need to give the older youth jobs and a place that they can go to talk about different issues. We have to give them something in which they can look up to an older person or someone they can talk to. Our children's mindset today is terrible. We have to give them the right things to go on. I remember when I was coming up as a young kid we had people that would sit us down and talk to us about different things or holler at us if we did something wrong. It is not like that today. Our children are running wild because they don't have anyone to talk to or they don't have jobs to go to. These are the things that we need to work on. We need to give them something back. We created these problems in our city and in our children. These problems didn't start because of the children. These problems were already in place when most of them were born into this world. When we look at the young generation that is on the street and doing bad things, it is because they don't have the attention that they need. If a child is doing something out of the ordinary most of the time they are doing it because they want attention. Negative attention is better than no attention at all for some. What they do today in the streets is because we as adults are a big part in that we set the precedent for them. They see us participating in negative things and acting out bad behaviors. They see adults doing drugs, drinking alcohol, having unprotected sex and they repeat these same negative behaviors. They need us adults to stop them when they are doing something bad and let them know that there is a better way to get what they want out of life and give them a hug. We need programs to educate the community and teach them how to live. We need educational programs that will teach trades, nutrition and how to take care of their temples.   We need to build up our youth and put time into them and work with them. This is what they need to keep their minds active and keep them occupied. For instance at 42nd and Girard there is a Bill Gates school that teaches our children about computers. This is what we need more of in our city. That is why I say we need money to clean up the violence in the city via way of programs to get the children involved in other things. I remember when there were gang wars. Guys were fighting and not shooting, now there is more shooting. It is all around you. The talk on the street today is about guns and money.

Hart VS Hayward

This is why I promote boxing and get the youth involved. When you participate in boxing you begin to get serious about your mind and body. You have to eat right, get the proper nutrition, the right amount of sleep and you have to live right. This helps condition your body and your mind. You also see the results which helps build self-esteem. Football and basketball also brings out a lot of good things in our youth and helps them generate a body that is healthy. We have to deal with our generation of youth on a sports level to promote overall health. You are what you eat and training helps them stay focused on eating the right foods. I remember reading in a book that if you eat the wrong foods you start thinking like the foods that you eat. All the junk food that our youth are eating is not good for them. They stay up all night long and don't get the proper rest and can't focus on school. We need to work on these things to promote better health in our youth. In time we can do this if we work together. It can't be just about conversation, we need action. Boxers that are still in the industry see the same thing I see when the guys come in the gym. Mr. Bobby "Boogaloo" Watts is still in the gym and training young boxers for the sport. He is giving back what he knows how to do well. I am doing what I can to give something back to create something better for them. We are in the gym everyday with these kids. We know how they think, how they feel. You see a kid come in the gym everyday and you see them develop to be a good fighter and everyone wants to be a part of this. So we are doing something to help the community that we live in. Now we have a lot of kids from the community coming into the gym and see the other kids growing and becoming successful in the things that we are putting in them and helping to develop in them, this will bring other kids out of the street and into the gym and give them an opportunity to clean up their lives.

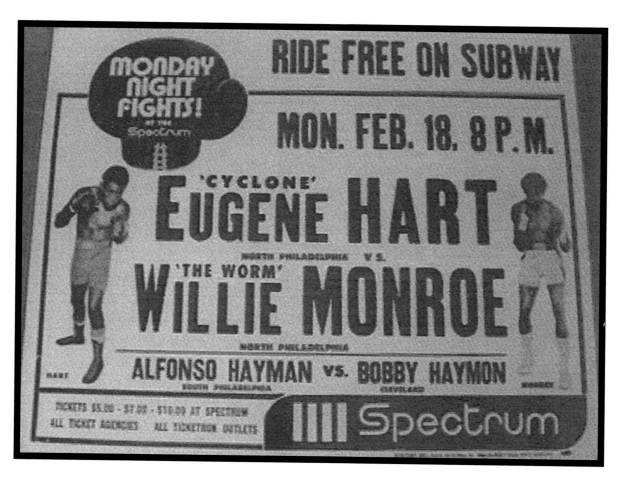

Hart VS Monroe

All of these drugs going on in our community is about money. Our kids get a taste of the big fast money, going back and forth to jail, able to live the good life while they have it, seeing that money can do this or get them that. What the people who live in the big houses on the hill need to see is that what got us in trouble is money and what's going to bring us out of trouble is money. We need more money to put into our programs to build and develop our communities up. It is not going to get done off of conversation. It takes money to make things happen in our community. This is what they took out of our community – money. That is how they move up on those big hills in Jersey and over in Delaware. The money went out of the city. Now we have to put the money back in the city for the little people.

This is my life story and it is a part of me. It hits my heart overwhelmingly because I know where I've been and where I am today. I am pleased to be where I am today in life. I want to dedicate my book to my family because of all the things I went through coming up as a child up until now, they know my history and have been there for me. I would like to see this book turn into a film and be taped right in the community in which I grew up. I also would like to Thank God for the things that I have been through in life. I want to thank the people who have been a great help to me. I want to thank Lucian Blackwell, the man who has been a great inspiration in my life, and his wife, Jannie Blackwell. I want to thank all of the politicians in the city that have done great things for me to help me along the way. Tommy Blackwell is doing a great job, Mayor John Street for giving me the chance to work with the youth at the Martin Luther King Recreation Center, Darryl Clark who is doing a great job in the community with our youth. Connie Little, the Mayors secretary who has also been a great help to me. I really appreciate the help they give me and hope they continue to help Mr. "Boogaloo" Watts, other fighters and myself to grow and help us with the programs for the youth so we can tackle this "War on Guns and Stop the Violence" in our city. May God Bless You All. Peace. *END OF SESSION IV:*

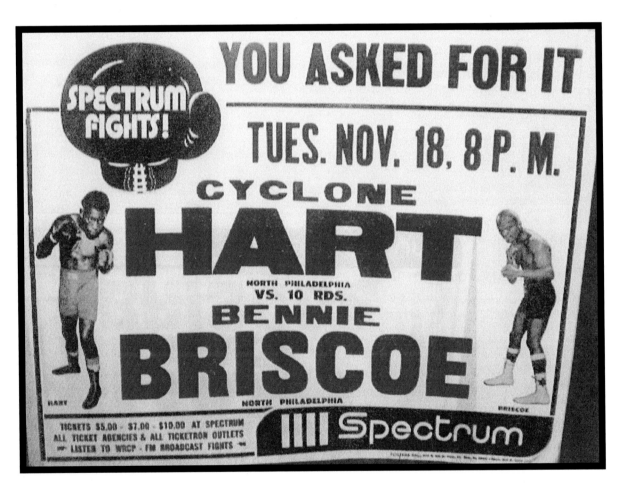

Hart VS Briscoe

Always dangerous, Hart lost major fights to Willie "The Worm" Monroe, Bobby "Boogaloo" Watts, Eddie Gregory (Mustafa Muhammad), Briscoe (in their rematch), Marvin Hagler and Vito Antuofermo. He scored some big wins himself, defeating Don Fullmer, Fate Davis, Matt Donovan (twice), Radames Cabrera, Mario Rosa, Sugar Ray Seales and Melvin Dennis. Hart, who turned pro at 17 in 1969, was 30-9 2, 28 Kos.

Who...Stanley "Kitten" Hayward
From...West Philadelphia
The Facts...What a character! Still is! Flamboyant Hayward was a charmer and a talker, but he could fight. His 1964 knockout of future world welterweight champion Curtis Cokes, in which he got off the deck in round two to stop Coke two rounds later on the old Friday Night Fights, is regarded a the greatest fight ever at the Blue Horizon. Hayward defeated Percy Manning, Dick Turner, Vince Shomo, Tito Marshall, Bennie Briscoe, Fate Davis, Pete Toro and Emile Griffith and he was ranked among the best at welterweight, junior middleweight and middleweight during his career, which ran from 1959 to 1977. He quit in 1971 after Eugene "Cyclone" Hart Kod him in one round, but came back more than two years later and made some noise, beating Li'l Abner and giving Briscoe fits in a losing cause in their long-awaited rematch. Hayward was 32-12-4, 18 Kos. Went to work in City Hall after retirement and he's a hit there, too.

Eugene Cyclone Hart

Cyclone Hart lands an early-round right before losing to Marv Hagler on a TKO in the 9th round

Hart VS Hagler

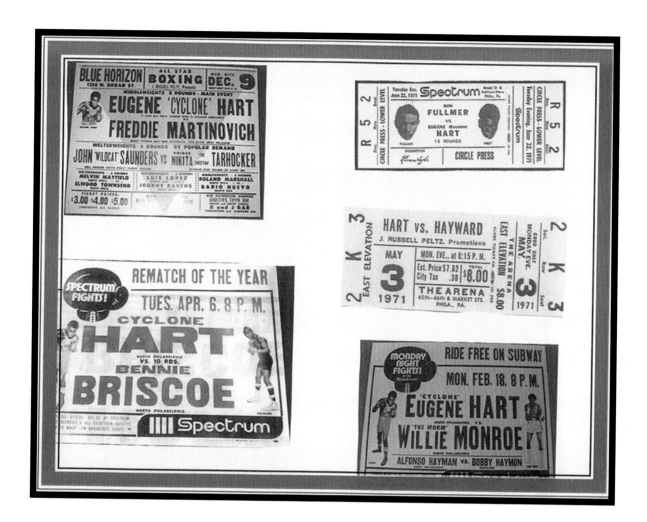

Tickets & Posters

Friday Nite Fights

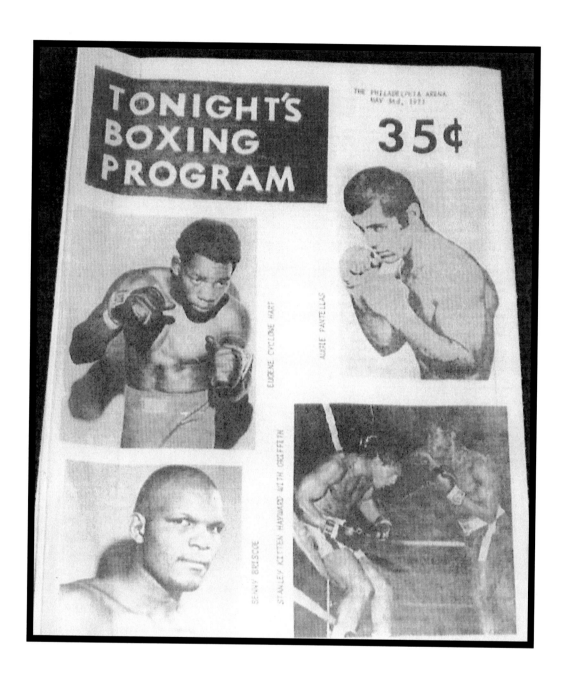

Boxing Program

Printed in the United States
by Baker & Taylor Publisher Services